FIESTA!

POLAND

GROLIER

Reprinted 2002
First printed in 1999 by Grolier Educational
Sherman Turnpike, Danbury, Connecticut.
Copyright © 1999 Times Editions Pte Ltd. Singapore.

Set ISBN: 0-7172-9324-6
Volume ISBN: 0-7172-9336-X

CIP information available from the Library of Congress or the publisher

Brown Partworks Ltd.

Series Editor: Tessa Paul
Series Designer: Joyce Mason
Crafts devised and created by Susan Moxley
Music arrangements by Harry Boteler
Photographs by Bruce Mackie
Subeditor: Annette Cheyne
Production: Alex Mackenzie
Stylists: Joyce Mason and Tessa Paul

For this volume:
Writer: Paul Thompson
Consultant: Anna Walczak
Editorial Assistants: Hannah Beardon and Paul Thompson

Printed in Italy

Adult supervision advised for all crafts and recipes,
particularly those involving sharp instruments and heat.

CONTENTS

POLAND:

Poland is situated in the north of central Europe. It has borders with many countries and forms a bridge between Western and Eastern Europe.

Germany

Czech Republic

▲**The Column of Sigismund III Vasa** stands in Castle Square in the Polish capital of Warsaw. It was erected in memory of the king who moved the capital from Kraków to Warsaw, and it is over 70 feet high.

First Impressions

- **Population** 38,544,000
- **Largest city** Warsaw with a population of 1,655,700
- **Longest river** Vistula
- **Highest mountain** Mt. Rysy at 8,199 ft.
- **Exports** Coal, copper, sulfur, machinery, meat, vehicles, chemicals, and forest products
- **Capital city** Warsaw
- **Political status** Republic
- **Climate** Warm summers, cold and snowy winters
- **Art and culture** Famous for the dance called the Polka, the composer Frederick Chopin, and the poet Adam Mickiewicz. Poland has also produced many great musicians, among them the pianist Artur Rubinstein.

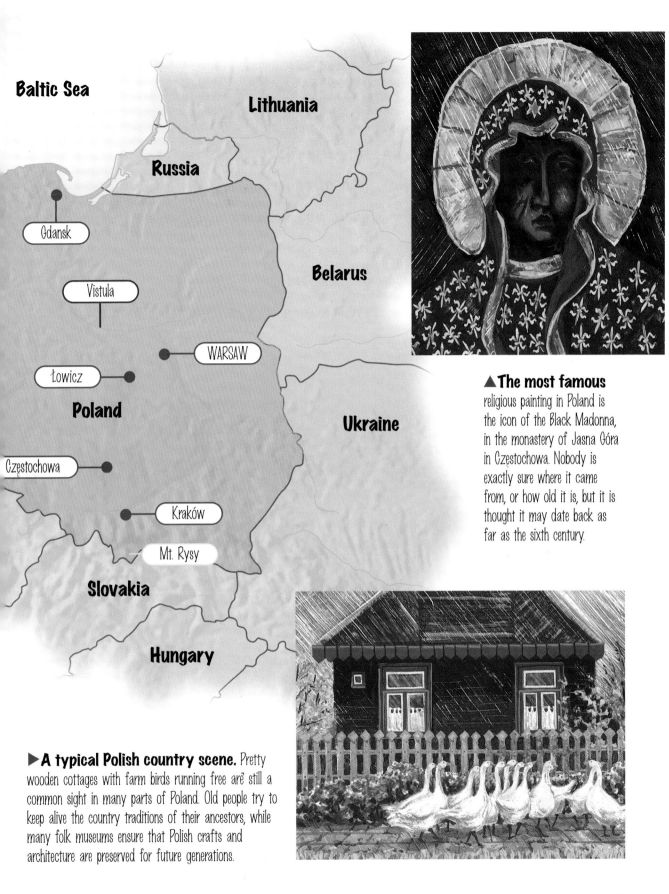

Baltic Sea

Lithuania

Russia

Belarus

Gdansk

Vistula

WARSAW

Łowicz

Poland

Ukraine

Częstochowa

Kraków

Mt. Rysy

Slovakia

Hungary

▲The most famous religious painting in Poland is the icon of the Black Madonna, in the monastery of Jasna Góra in Częstochowa. Nobody is exactly sure where it came from, or how old it is, but it is thought it may date back as far as the sixth century.

▶A typical Polish country scene. Pretty wooden cottages with farm birds running free are still a common sight in many parts of Poland. Old people try to keep alive the country traditions of their ancestors, while many folk museums ensure that Polish crafts and architecture are preserved for future generations.

RELIGIONS

Christianity is the religion of Poland, and the vast majority of people are Roman Catholic. Many Polish traditions and festivals are connected to the religious calendar and its ceremonies.

CHRISTIANS believe in the teachings of Jesus, who was born in the Middle East about 2,000 years ago. They believe that Jesus was the Son of God.

Christianity came to Poland in 966 A.D. When the Catholic Church faced division during the fourteenth and fifteenth centuries, most Poles stayed loyal to the pope and the Catholic Church.

In the eighteenth century Poland was divided up by the powerful nations of Europe. However, even though the state of Poland no longer existed, the Christian faith of the Polish people and their belief in their own culture kept the Polish nation alive. Poland was again recognized as an independent state in the nineteenth century.

For centuries Poland was home to the largest population of Jews in Europe. However, during World War II Poland was taken over by Nazi Germany. The Nazis sent the Jews to concentration camps, and very few Jewish people survived these terrible places.

At the end of this war in 1945 Poland was no longer independent. The country was then ruled by Russia, which installed a Communist system. In such a system the state owns all the businesses and farms. Private firms or landowners are not allowed.

Many Poles were very unhappy with this system. Eventually, however, with help from the Roman Catholic Church they regained control of their country in 1989. Poland now rules itself and is a democracy.

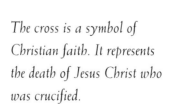

The cross is a symbol of Christian faith. It represents the death of Jesus Christ who was crucified.

GREETINGS FROM **POLAND!**

Poland is one of the largest countries in central Europe. It came into existence over 1,000 years ago when the Piasts, the first ruling family of Poland, came into power. In 1793 Poland lost its independence, and Germany, Austria-Hungary, and Russia ruled the country for over 100 years. During World War II almost 20 percent of the Polish population died under German and Russian occupation.

Even under foreign rule the Polish kept their culture, language, and religion alive. Polish is a Slavonic language and uses the Roman alphabet.

How do you say...

Hello
Cześć

How are you?
Jak się masz?

My name is...
Moje imię...

Goodbye
Do widzenia

Thank you
Dziękuję

Peace
Pokój

DROWNING MARZANNA

Forty days before Easter is a time of fasting called Lent. The church has no festivals, but a ritual that is not Christian occurs in rural places. It is called "Drowning Marzanna."

On the fourth Sunday of Lent crowds of people, some of them in traditional costume, gather on the riverbanks of Poland. They bring with them large, stuffed dolls. These are the *Marzannas.* Some may be straw scarecrows, some may be rag dolls made of fabric. The Marzanna dolls are clothed in traditional costumes like those worn by the women in the crowd.

Groups of people form a circle around a doll, and they all sing songs about the departure of the cold winter weather that will allow the spring to arrive. They throw the Marzanna into the river, and this act symbolizes the death of winter.

There are other beliefs connected to the Marzanna. In

Eggs symbolize new life and growth. Painted eggs are given to children after the drowning of the Marzanna. These eggs are also used as gifts at Easter time.

In medieval times women accused of witch-craft were often drowned. The Marzanna represents a witch of death and winter. To weaken her power she is never given a face.

parts of Poland the crowds hurry home after the drowning of the doll. They think it unlucky to speak or to look back. Some even believe that to fall or trip on the way home means they might die within the year.

Drowning Marzanna is a very old tradition. Its roots are found in the fears of early farmers who dreaded the long, dark winters found in northern Europe. They were very happy when the sun appeared. This ritual is not so wide-spread now, but it still takes place in little towns and remote villages of Poland.

Nowadays drowning Marzanna is a light-hearted event, often celebrated as part of school activities.

GAIK – SYMBOL OF LIFE

The branch of a fir tree decorated with ribbons, painted eggs, and feathers is also brought to the gathering. This branch is called a *gaik*. It symbolizes the rebirth of the sun and is believed to bring new life into a village, while the drowning of the doll is said to drive out death and protect the inhabitants from sickness. After the Marzanna, a symbol of winter and death, is thrown into the river, the gaik is paraded around the village, accompanied by groups of singers. Sometimes girls carry the gaik from door to door. Everywhere they stop they are given presents of painted eggs.

WIELKI TYDZIEŃ

As in other Christian countries the week before Easter, Holy Week, is an important time in Poland. People follow certain rituals to recall the crucifixion and resurrection of Christ.

Holy Week, or *Wielki Tydzień*, in Poland is a time of both fasting and of celebration. The week begins with the rituals of Palm Sunday, which is the day Jesus rode into Jerusalem on a donkey. Crowds of people welcomed Him by waving palm leaves.

On Palm Sunday people carry branches of pussy willow to church to represent the palm leaves. In some places willow branches are laid down on the floor of the church for the priest to walk over. In other parts of Poland the palms are artistic designs of dried flowers and dyed grass.

On Good Friday each church displays a model of the tomb where Christ was buried. People go from church to church to admire the artistry of these models.

On Saturday people take a basket of food to the church to be blessed. The baskets hold

On Holy Saturday people take lambs made of sugar or straw to be blessed. The lamb represents Christ, who in the Christian religion is sometimes called the Lamb of God.

pisanki, or "painted eggs," a lamb made of sugar or straw, bread, sausages, and cakes.

Easter Sunday is the day when Jesus

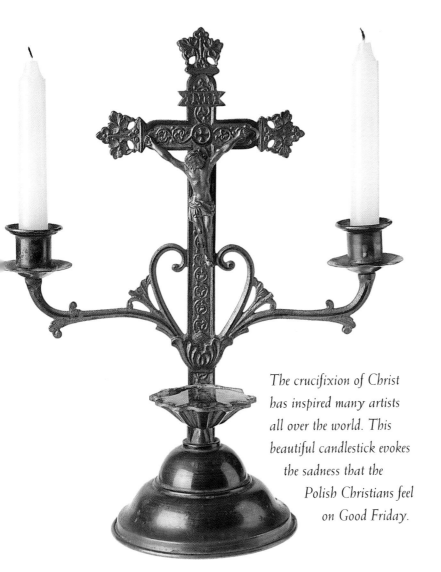

The crucifixion of Christ has inspired many artists all over the world. This beautiful candlestick evokes the sadness that the Polish Christians feel on Good Friday.

sprinkling water over each other. *Dyngus* means "ransom." In exchange for a promise not to throw water at them, girls give boys a ransom of Easter eggs or candies. People who get wet in this way are happy. It is supposed to bring luck and a good harvest. If a boy throws water at a girl, it means he likes her!

In the east of Poland people roll a circular cake called *korowaj* around their fields to keep evil away and bring good luck.

came back to life – the Resurrection. On this day nobody can sleep late because boys wake up early and race through the streets setting off toy explosive devices. The noise they make is supposed to resemble the noise of the stone rolling away from Christ's tomb.

Easter Sunday also marks the end of Lenten fasting, so when people return from church they enjoy a big breakfast of eggs, meat, and cakes.

Dyngus, the term for Easter Monday, is also a day of joy. Everyone has fun

After the Easter Sunday breakfast traditional cakes are served, such as this cake called a baba.

BOŻE CIAŁO

Boże Ciało *means "the body of Christ." The words describe an important feast day, usually known as* Corpus Christi, *in the Catholic Church.*

In the Christian faith there is a deeply significant ritual called Mass, or Holy Communion. It recalls Christ's last supper, and holy bread and wine are a central part of the ritual.

The feast of *Boże Ciało,* or *Corpus Christi,* affirms the Catholic belief that Christ Himself is present in the bread and wine.

The Corpus Christi procession plays an important part. These parades take place in towns and villages across Poland, but the most famous is held in the central town of Łowicz.

This begins with a Mass that takes place in the main public square. The Mass is

followed by a slow procession around the square. The women are dressed in beautiful traditional costumes. They hold ribbons attached to banners held upright. These

On Corpus Christi people bring wreaths of herbs to the churches to be blessed and used as medicine. The women in the procession wear embroidered costumes such as the one on this doll.

The bread and wine of Holy Communion is sacred. To honor their holy role, the wafers of bread may be served on a gold plate, and the wine sipped from a gem-studded, gold chalice.

Religious paintings on wood are called icons. They can be seen in many Polish churches.

are embroidered with the figure of Christ, the Virgin Mary, or scenes from the Bible.

Behind the women are boys in new clothes and girls dressed in white. These children are to receive their First Communion. This means they will take the bread and wine for the first time.

When the procession returns to the church on the square, there is a short service and then everyone parades back to their own local church.

SHELTERED ALTARS

In every town and village in Poland people work together to construct small shelters for the Corpus Christi celebrations. Under these shelters they prepare altars to be used for worship on Corpus Christi. Statues or paintings of saints are placed on the altars and decorated with foliage or small birch trees, and with flowers, ribbons, and embroidered fabrics.

In the religions of ancient times altars were commonly used for the offering of a sacrificial animal. These altars were built outside the temple. However, in the Christian church they moved inside and became the focus of ritual. By tradition they were located at the east end of the church. Over the centuries altars have changed from a simple structure of a slab resting on two legs to magnificent tables of worship. They are ornamented with carvings and precious crucifixes, and covered with embroidered silk cloths.

MAKE A PAPER PALM

On Palm Sunday Christians carry branches of palm or crosses made of palm leaves. In Poland some people carry paper decorations that symbolize palm branches.

Palm trees do not grow in Poland, so instead willow branches are carried by many believers. However, in the villages of Rabka, Tokarnia, and Lyse the "palms" are works of art made from colorful paper flowers. Make your own version of these symbolic palm-tree branches.

YOU WILL NEED
Colored crepe paper
Thread
Wooden pole about 24" long

1 Take a roll of crepe paper and cut through the roll, dividing it into small rolls each about 5" wide. Unroll one of these and cut into strips each about 7" long. Repeat with each 5" roll. You should have several strips of crepe paper 5" x 7".

2 Put three strips on top of each other and pleat them. Tie a thread 12" long around the middle of the pleated strips. Open and flatten the pleats each side of the tie. When you have four flowers, tie them to the pole, using the thread tied round their middles.

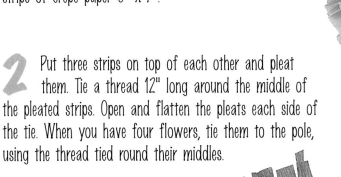

3 To make the leaves, cut a strip of green crepe paper 5" x 9". Fold it in half along the length and snip a fringe on the open edge. Tie on to the pole at the center fold. Continue covering the pole with flowers and leaves. At the top wind a strip of leaf paper around the pole with snipped edge facing upwards. Wind a strip of paper around the lower end of the stick. Attach crepe paper ribbons to the top.

LAJKONIK

*A week after Corpus Christi a colorful pageant called **Lajkonik** takes place in the city of Kraków. It is held in remembrance of a raid by the Tartars, whom the people of Kraków defeated.*

The pageant begins at about 2:30 at the Norbertine monastery just outside the center of Kraków. Several people dressed in costumes enter the monastery courtyard accompanied by a band that is called the *mlaskoty*. They are followed by the Lajkonik. This is a comical character dressed to look like a Tartar on horseback. The Tartars came from Mongolia, a country in the Far East. They invaded Poland in the thirteenth century. Lajkonik was a brave waterman who killed a Tartar, stole his costume, and rode into the city of Kraków to announce the defeat of the Tartars. During the pageant Lajkonik enters the courtyard to a loud fanfare of trumpets. In one hand he carries a straw basket and a wooden mace in the other.

People dressed in costumes of the Polish nobility open the celebrations in the monastery courtyard. Some of the men and women in the crowd wear the local costume of Kraków, which is also the national costume of Poland.

Every time someone puts money into the basket, Lakjonik taps their shoulder with the mace as a sign of good luck.

After visiting the nuns and priests of the monastery, Lajkonik leads the procession toward the town. He stops on the way at a restaurant named after him. Finally he reaches the main square and performs a dance. The leaders of the city then present him with a reward for killing the Tartar.

Dolls and toys are modeled on the triumphant Lajkonik in his stolen Tartar costume – a reminder of the waterman's defeat of the Tartars. During the procession Lajkonik stops for a bite to eat and is offered these traditional Polish cookies.

17

THE STORY OF THE "HEJNAŁ"

The bravery of a trumpeter once saved the people of Kraków from the Tartars. To this day, a tune called "Hejnał" pays tribute to his courage.

THERE IS A CHURCH in the city of Kraków called the Church of our lady. It is a very beautiful old Gothic church with two towers. One of these is bigger than the other. From the taller of the two towers, a trumpeter sounds the hour with a tune called "Hejnał."

A legend about these towers explains the unusual difference in size. They were built by two brothers. The brother who started to build the narrower tower was jealous, thinking that his brother's tower would be higher and more beautiful. He killed his brother. Then he finished both towers and made the wider one lower and plainer.

One day a long time ago, when Eastern Europe lived in fear of the Tartars, the trumpeter was looking out from his tower. In the distance he saw something strange. It looked like a cloud of dust. Gradually, he realized it was a Tartar army galloping toward Kraków.

What could he do? How could he warn the people of Kraków? Quickly he took up his trumpet and began to play the "Hejnał" over and over again. At first, the citizens of Kraków thought this was very strange. What is wrong with the trumpeter, they thought, why is he doing that? Soon, however, they realized that something was seriously wrong. They knew it could

only mean the trumpeter was trying to warn them that the Tartars were coming.

The men of Kraków locked up their families and took up their weapons. One of the Tartars galloping toward the city saw the trumpeter in the tower trying to warn the people. This Tartar took his bow and arrow and shot the trumpeter, hitting him in the throat and killing him. The trumpeter's tune stopped all of a sudden, and the people of Kraków knew he must have been killed. The Tartars must be near the city, they thought. Thanks to the warning, they were well prepared to fight the Tartars off and drive the enemy away.

To this day, the "Hejnal" is played in Kraków every hour and stops suddenly unfinished – in remembrance of the trumpeter who saved the city from the Tartars. People all over Poland can hear the "Hejnal" at noon every day on Polish radio, transmitted directly from the tower.

HARVEST FESTIVAL

The harvest is the culmination of a great deal of work for farmers. Country people celebrate the seasonal end to their labor with happy festivities.

From the beginning of August people in farming communities begin the work of harvesting crops. This work is extremely tiring, and when it is finished, everyone celebrates. They also want to thank God for the food He provided.

The celebrations start with a man and a young woman being chosen to represent all the harvesters. The woman is dressed in a folk costume. She wears a crown woven from wheat straws and flowers. The man, who is often older than the girl, is also in traditional clothes.

To show off the harvest, large wreaths are made of wheat, rye, and flowers.

The chosen couple carry the wreath and lead a procession into the center of the town or village. Here they are greeted by the head of the town council or village committee. In the past the head was usually either a wealthy landowner or one of the nobility.

In the autumn Harvest Festivals are held in the churches. The villagers decorate the church and arrange colorful displays of fruits and vegetables in front of the altar.

PLACKI ZIEMNIACZANE

Grate the potato in a food processor. Squeeze out as much water as you can. Mix the potato, onions, salt, pepper, and eggs together. If the mixture looks runny, add ¼ cup flour.

Heat 1 T. of oil in a large frying pan. With a large spoon, drop some of the mixture into the oil. Flatten with a spatula. Cook on both sides until the inside is soft, and the outside is brown and crisp. Use up all the batter to make the pancakes, adding more oil as needed, and serve hot with sour cream and apple sauce.

TO SERVE SIX
1 large potato, peeled
½ onion, diced
¼ cup flour (optional)
2 eggs
2 T. oil
1 t. salt
¼ t. pepper

The man and woman carrying the wreath present it to the head of the town, who is usually the mayor. Sometimes the woman is given a coral necklace by the mayor in exchange for the harvest wreath.

These presentations are followed by a big party for the whole village. Harvest songs are sung, and people dance the Polonez, or "Polonaise," a solemn dance that opens the celebrations and balls all over Poland.

Partygoers enjoy a festive meal, dance, and are happy the harvest is over and the crops successfully gathered in.

In some places there is a ritual to the cutting of the last bunch of grain. People sing while the bunch is cut with a sickle. Then they decorate it with flowers and ribbons, or weave it into a braid. It may be saved until Christmas when it serves as a decoration.

21

ŚWIĘTO WNIEBOWZIĘCIA

Święto Wniebowzięcia *means the Feast of the Assumption, the day when the Virgin Mary was taken up to heaven.*

In the middle of August almost one million pilgrims arrive at Jasna Góra in the country town of Częstochowa. This, Jasna Góra, is the most famous monastery in Poland. A monastery is a place where monks live and work. The people make this trip to remember Mary, the mother of Jesus, and show their respect for her. Some of them walk to the monastery all the way from Warsaw, a journey that takes nine days.

People who travel to holy places for religious reasons are called pilgrims. Many of the pilgrims who travel to Jasna Góra wear traditional dress on this day, *Święto Wniebowzięcia*, when Mary rose in both body

As the mother of Jesus Christ Mary is especially important to all Roman Catholics. On August 15 women carry embroidered hearts to express their sympathy with Mary's grief over her son's death.

Processions are held in many places on Assumption Day. Women carry crowns to show Mary is the queen of heaven and all the saints.

and soul to heaven to be with God.

Jasna Góra houses a beautiful icon of the Virgin Mary called the Black Madonna. It is said to hold miraculous powers that have protected the monks and their monastery from invasion in times of war. There are other legends about the icon of the Black Madonna. One of them tells of unruly soldiers who tried to slash her face with their swords. Another story claims that the wonderful picture was painted on Mary's kitchen table by Saint Luke the Evangelist.

All over Poland processions take place on the Feast of the Assumption. Women dress in bridal gowns in imitation of the purity of the Virgin. Bunches of flowers are carried by the faithful.

A copy of the icon of the Black Madonna is paraded through the streets. Beautiful banners with religious images are held high above the crowd.

MOTHER OF HERBS

On August 15 women take bunches of herbs such as sage, thyme, and dill to church to have them blessed. This old tradition goes back to a time when people believed that blessing the herbs gave the plants special powers. Sometimes these herbs were put under the roofs of houses to protect them from lightning. Often they were used to make natural remedies. The importance of herbs in Poland is reflected in the popular Polish name for Assumption Day — *Matki Boskiej Zielnej*, meaning "the day of the Blessed Mother of the Herbs."

THE LEGEND OF THE PIASTS

The Piasts were simple folk who were kind to strangers.
Their generosity was rewarded. Their son became king,
and the family then ruled Poland for 400 years.

LONG AGO, when all Poland suffered under the evil king Popiel, two travelers visited the country. After walking for days, they were very tired. When at last they reached some city gates, the travelers were turned away by guards who said: "Where are you from? You ought to know today is a great royal celebration. This is the day the sons of a prince are to have their heads shaved."

Shaving boys' heads was a tradition in Poland before the country became Christian. When a boy reached the age of seven, a banquet would be held. The most important guest at the banquet would shave the boy's head. The boy would then be given another name and would join the company of men.

The two travelers begged to be allowed in, but the guards accused them of being thieves. The tired travelers sadly turned away. Eventually they came to a small village. In front of one of the cottages stood a man. He was dressed poorly, but he looked like an honest man. He asked them if they would like to rest in his humble cottage. They gladly accepted the man's hospitality. The man's name was Piast.

Inside they met the man's wife, Rzepicha, and his son who had also reached the age of seven. But the family was poor, and its celebrations were going to be very simple.

The travelers were given wine and pork. It was the food reserved to celebrate the shaving. Piast was amazed to see that the bottle of wine never became empty, nor did the pork ever finish. He realized his mysterious visitors were unusual men.

One of the guests shaved the boy's head. The Piasts did not know that the guest was an important prince. They simply obeyed when this traveler told Piast to name the boy Ziemowit. Then the travelers vanished. Kindly old Piast knew something special had happened to his family that day.

Something special happened to all Poland after this visit. King Popiel was eaten alive by mice for his evil doings. Ziemowit grew to be such a brave, wise knight that the people made him king, and he proved a wise ruler of Poland.

Boże Narodzenie

Boże Narodzenie *means Christmas. In Poland, this festival begins on December 24 and continues until January 6. It is a joyful season to celebrate the birth of Jesus Christ.*

The Polish Christmas season begins with Christmas Eve on December 24. Every year, Polish children eagerly look forward to the two-week holiday and celebration. Polish children are also likely to receive many gifts at this time of year.

In Kraków, there is a tradition of making models of the birth of Baby Jesus in the stable. They are called *szopki*, and the stables are made to look like churches. A competition is held for the best szopka.

The most important day of the festival is Christmas Eve. In Poland, this is called *Wigilia*. The word derives from the Latin *vigilare*, the meaning of which is "to watch." This is the day for family visits and the giving and receiving of gifts.

Poles eat a meal that

JEZUS MALUSIEŃKI

Je - zus Ma - lu - sien - ki   Le - zy wsrod sta - jen - ki

I drzy z zim - na,   wzdy - cha nad Nim   to ser - ce Ma - ten - ki.

A u - bo - ga   by - la   Ra - bek z glo - wy   zdje - la,

W kto-ry Dzie - cie   U - wi - naws - zy,   Sian - kiem Je   ok - ry - la.

includes fish but not meat, as Wigilia is a day for fasting. The Poles have a tradition of hospitality, so they prepare an extra place at the table in case a guest arrives.

After the Wigilia meal, people go to church for Midnight Mass to celebrate the birth of Jesus.

JESUS, TINY BABY

Little Jesus lay in the stable Shivering with cold; His Mother whispered.
She was poor, so she took her shawl from her head, Wrapped the Baby and covered Him with hay.

The szopki — models of the birth of Christ in a stable — include wood carvings of the Holy Family and the stable animals.

MAKE A PAPER CUT-OUT

In the long winters country people amused themselves by cutting paper into shapes and pictures. Their skills led to the development of a distinctive form of folk art.

The craft of making paper cut-outs began in the nineteenth century, and they were made by the peasants who farmed the land. Their designs were taken from familiar elements of life in the country. Flowers, fruits, animals, and birds were fashioned by these craftsmen. Copy a traditional pattern or create your own design.

YOU WILL NEED
Colored paper
Tracing paper
Pencil
Cardboard
Glue

1 Draw and color your design on paper. If you are doing a symmetrical design, you need only to draw one half. Start with the biggest cut-out shape in your design. Fold the colored paper and trace your design on the reverse side. Line up the center line of the design shape with the fold.

2 Cut out your shape and paste it onto the cardboard. Trace and cut out the smaller shapes. Paste them on the cardboard according to your design. If you are doing symmetrical shapes, make sure the colored paper is folded before tracing the shape onto the paper.

3 As you cut out the shapes, paste them into the right place. If you are making an animal design, use a hole punch to make paper dots for eyes. When you have finished, you can frame your craft or make a card from it.

ZADUSZKI

Zaduszki *is All Soul's Day. It is a day to honor the souls of the dead. Christians visit the graves of their dead relatives. Candles are lit, flowers are placeed on many graves, and the dead are even served meals.*

On the evening of November 1, the eve of Zaduszki, or All Souls' Day, Christians place candles and flowers on family graves. It is an old belief that on this day, the dead come back to visit Earth. Special foods are made for these visitors, such as rye bread made in the shape of a body.

Families join in a special meal. Food is laid for the dead relatives. All Souls' Day is also a time to be charitable to the living and to give food to the hungry and homeless.

On the eve of Zaduszki, cemeteries across Poland are lit by candles flickering in glass jars.

WORDS TO KNOW

Altar: A table on which worshippers leave offerings, burn incense, or perform ceremonies.

Communism: A method of running a country in which all property is owned by the government. Under Communism people supposedly work at the job they are best able to do and are paid according to their needs.

Democracy: A system of government in which the people choose their leaders by voting in elections.

Icon: A religious picture or image.

Fast: To go without some or all kinds of food and drink deliberately.

Lent: The 40 days between Ash Wednesday and Easter.

Mace: A decorated staff, or pole.

Mass: A Christian ritual in which bread and wine are used to commemorate the Last Supper of Jesus Christ.

Medieval: To do with the Middle Ages, the period between the fifth and the fifteenth centuries.

Monastery: A place where monks live in a religious community.

Nazi: A political party that governed Germany between 1933 and 1945. The Nazis invaded much of Europe and killed millions of Jews, Gypsies, and Catholics in death camps.

Pilgrim: A person who makes a religious journey, or pilgrimage, to a holy place.

Ransom: The price paid for the release of a captured person or object.

Resurrection: The rising of Christ from the dead on Easter Sunday.

Roman Catholic: A member of the Roman Catholic Church, the largest branch of Christianity. The head of this church is the pope.

Saint: A title given to very holy people by some Christian churches. Saints are important in the Roman Catholic Church.

ACKNOWLEDGMENTS

WITH THANKS TO:
The Polish Institute and Sikorski Museum, London. Pollock's Toy Museum, London. Vale Antiques, London. Embroidered heart and Marzanna doll by Zoë Paul.

PHOTOGRAPHY:
All photographs by Bruce Mackie except: John Elliott p. 28. Cover photograph by Image Bank/Wendy Chan.

ILLUSTRATIONS BY:
Fiona Saunders pp. 4 – 5. Tracy Rich p. 7. Fiona Saunders p. 17. Maps by John Woolford.

Recipes: Ellen Dupont.

SET CONTENTS